SCHOLASTIC

News

Nonfiction Readers

A Kangaroo Joey Grows Up

by Katie Marsico

Children's Press®
A Division of Scholastic Inc.
New York Toronto London Auckland Sydney
g Kong
Danbury, Connecticut

These content vocabulary word builders are for grades 1–2.

Subject Consultant: Susan H. Gray, MS, Zoology

Reading Consultant: Cecilia Minden-Cupp, PhD, Former Director of the Language and Literacy Program, Harvard Graduate School of Education, Cambridge, Massachusetts

Photographs © 2007: Alamy Images/Arco Images: 23 top right; Dembinsky Photo Assoc./Skip Moody: 5 top right, 12 right; Getty Images: 1, 4 bottom right, 7, 20 top right, 21 bottom left, 21 top left (Howie Garber/The Image Bank), 17, 21 top right (Frank Krahmer/The Image Bank); Minden Pictures: 23 bottom left (Jean-Paul Ferrero/Auscape), cover left inset, 5 bottom, 9, 10, 11, 20 center left, 20 top left (Mitsuaki Iwago), cover center inset, 4 bottom left, 13, 20 bottom right (Frans Lanting); Nature Picture Library Ltd.: 5 top left, 12 left (Bartussek/Arco), 23 bottom right (Dave Watts); NHPA/Dave Watts: back cover, 2, 4 top, 19, 23 top left; Peter Arnold Inc./Ruoso Cyril: cover right inset, 15, 21 center right; Superstock, Inc./age fotostock: cover background.

Book Design: Simonsays Design!
Book Production: The Design Lab

Library of Congress Cataloging-in-Publication Data
Marsico, Katie, 1980–
A Kangaroo Joey grows up / by Katie Marsico.
   p. cm. — (Scholastic news nonfiction readers)
Includes bibliographical references.
ISBN-13: 978-0-531-17476-0
ISBN-10: 0-531-17476-X
1. Kangaroos—Growth—Juvenile literature. 2.Kangaroos Development—
   Juvenile literature. I. Title. II. Series.
QL737.M35M274 2007
599.2'22—dc22   2006023798

1 2 3 4 5 6 7 8 9 10 R 16 15 14 13 12 11 10 09 08 07

CONTENTS

WORD HUNT

Look for these words as you read. They will be in **bold**.

adult
(**ah**-duhlt)

joey
(**jo**-ee)

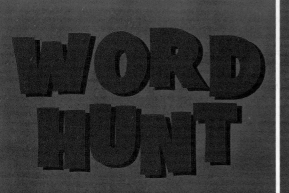

mammal
(**mam**-uhl)

4

dingoes
(**din**-goze)

hawks
(hoks)

nurses
(**nurs**-uhs)

pouch
(powch)

5

Joeys!

What's that bouncing in the air? It's a **joey**!

A joey is a baby kangaroo.

A kangaroo is a **mammal**. Mammals are animals whose babies drink milk from their mother's bodies.

How does a joey grow?

Kangaroos, like most mammals, have hair or fur.

Most kangaroos have just one baby at a time.

Newborn joeys are tiny. Many are only about 1 inch (2.5 centimeters) long!

The newborns have no hair. They can't see or hear very well.

A newborn joey doesn't look like a grown-up kangaroo.

A newborn joey climbs into a pocket on its mother's belly. This pocket is called a **pouch**.

A mother kangaroo **nurses** its joey when it is inside her pouch.

pouch

A mother kangaroo feeds her baby milk from her body, or nurses.

A joey keeps warm inside the pouch.

It is safe from enemies such as **hawks** and wild dogs called **dingoes**.

A joey usually doesn't leave the pouch for about six to eight months.

dingoes   hawk

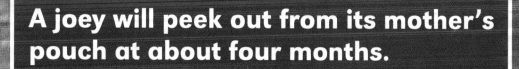

A joey will peek out from its mother's pouch at about four months.

13

At six to eight months, a joey begins to explore the outside world!

A joey tries eating different grasses. It practices hopping up and down.

It also learns to watch out for enemies.

A mother kangaroo carefully watches over her joey after it leaves the pouch.

Even after a joey leaves its mother's pouch, it still returns to spend time there.

A joey continues to drink its mother's milk for several months.

When joeys are about one year old, they leave their mother's pouch for good.

An older joey doesn't always climb into its mother's pouch when it wants a drink of milk.

A joey becomes an **adult** kangaroo when it is about eighteen months old.

Soon it will be time for the new adults to take care of their own joeys!

Gray kangaroos can travel up to 30 feet (9 meters) in a single hop!

A KANGAROO JOEY GROWS UP!

1

This joey was just born. A newborn joey lives in its mother's pouch.

2

A joey must drink milk from its mother to grow healthy and strong.

3

At four months old, a curious joey peeks outside its mother's pouch.

6 Not gone for good! Joeys continue to spend some time in their mother's pouch until they are about one year old.

7 A joey becomes an adult kangaroo at eighteen months.

5 Joeys try eating different grasses, and they grow quicker and stronger.

4 Time to explore! Between six and eight months, a joey leaves the pouch.

21

YOUR NEW WORDS

adult (**ah**-duhlt) a grown-up person or fully grown animal

dingoes (**din**-goze) wild dogs that live in Australia

hawks (hoks) hunting birds with short, rounded wings and long tails

joey (**jo**-ee) a baby kangaroo

mammal (**mam**-uhl) an animal that nurses its babies

nurses (**nurs**-uhs) feeds a baby milk made in the mother's body

pouch (powch) a pocketlike body part that some animals use to carry their young

THESE ANIMALS GROW UP IN POUCHES, TOO!

koala

opossum

sugar glider

wombat

INDEX

FIND OUT MORE
Book:
Hewett, Joan, and Richard Hewett (photographer). *A Kangaroo Joey Grows Up.* Minneapolis: Carolrhoda Books, 2002.

Website:
Our Animals: On the Ground—Kangaroos
http://www.abc.net.au/schoolstv/animals/KANGAROOS.htm

MEET THE AUTHOR
Katie Marsico lives with her family outside of Chicago, Illinois. She loves watching kangaroos at the local zoo and believes her daughter, Maria, probably spends as much time hopping up and down as a joey.